UNBEATABLE TEAMWORK

Viral infections, vascular troubles, allergies, diabetic cataracts and many other serious disorders have been found
to be helped by the powerful combination of vitamin C
and the bioflavonoids which are found in the white lining
of citrus-fruit rinds and other plants. Like C, they increase the immune defense against disease; together they
provide much more strength against inflammation than
each does separately. For half a century, research and
clinical data have recorded the good work of the bioflavonoids. Now they are beginning to receive the attention they deserve—and Jeffrey Bland is the nutrition ex-
pert who can tell their story.

ABOUT THE AUTHOR AND EDITORS

Jeffrey Bland, Ph.D., is a promoter of good health—whether he is teaching, practicing, lecturing or writing, he is actively committed to the idea that the relationship between health and lifestyle when properly revised leads to longer, healthier lives and more productive contributions to the survival of our species. A Ph.D. in biochemistry, he is Director of the Laboratory for Nutritional Supplement Analysis at the Linus Pauling Institute, and a dedicated advocate of healthful common sense from the lecture platform primarily to physicians, dentists and other scientists. His latest book is *Nutraerobics*, and he is editor of and contributor to *Medical Applications of Clinical Nutrition*.

Richard A. Passwater, Ph.D., is one of the most called-upon authorities for information relating to preventive health care. A noted biochemist, he is credited with popularizing the term "supernutrition," largely as a result of having written two bestsellers on the subject—*Supernutrition: Megavitamin Revolution* and *Supernutrition for Healthy Hearts*. His other books include *Easy No-Flab Diet*, *Cancer and Its Nutritional Therapies*, *Selenium as Food & Medicine* and the recently published *Hair Analysis* (with Elmer M. Cranton, M.D.).

Earl Mindell, R.Ph., Ph.D., combines the expertise and working experience of a pharmacist with extensive knowledge in most of the nutrition areas. His *Earl Mindell's Vitamin Bible* is now a million-copy bestseller; and his more recent *Vitamin Bible for Your Kids* may very well duplicate his first *Bible*'s publishing history. Dr. Mindell's popular *Quick & Easy Guide to Better Health* was recently published by Keats Publishing.

BIOFLAVONOIDS

THE FRIENDS AND HELPERS OF VITAMIN C
IN MANY HARD-TO-TREAT AILMENTS

by Jeffrey Bland, Ph.D

Keats Publishing, Inc. ✖ New Canaan, Connecticut

Bioflavonoids is not intended as medical advice. Its intention is solely informational and educational. Please consult a medical or health professional should the need for one be warranted.

Good Health Guides are published by Keats Publishing, Inc.
27 Pine Street (Box 876)
New Canaan, Connecticut 06840

Contents

Contents

INTRODUCTION

One of the most exciting chapters in the history of nutrition and medicine is the story of a pioneer investigator, Dr. Albert Szent-Györgyi, who was able in the 1930s to isolate from vegetable and fruit products a chemical substance capable of treating the disease scurvy. This antiscorbutic factor was named ascorbic acid and became known as vitamin C. Once isolated and chemically identified, it opened the door for the development forty years later of what is called orthomolecular medicine— the use of substances that are natural to the human body for the enhancement of physiological function.[1] Szent-Györgyi's work provided an explanation for the observation made almost two hundred years previously by Dr. James Lind, a British naval surgeon who found that scurvy could be prevented or treated by seamen if citrus fruits or juices were added to their diet on long voyages.

In a way, Dr. Lind was performing early orthomolecular therapy by using a natural substance, ascorbic acid, to treat a health problem related to a specific derangement in the body's metabolism. The term "orthomolecular" was coined by Dr. Linus Pauling to describe the use of natural substances—vitamins, minerals and other accessory nutrients—to help regulate metabolism and improve health. A key principle of orthomolecular therapy is to recognize each patient's biochemical individuality and to administer therapeutic nutrients on the basis of that individuality. It has to do not only with the use of vitamin C, but all other necessary nutrients, as well as natural substances found in the body, to help augment and support biochemical individuality. Vitamin C, as found in whole foods, is associated with many other natural products that may be considered orthomolecular substances.

Dr. Szent-Györgyi made one other important observation when working with natural products with antiscorbutic properties. He found that there were synergistic substances in these foods that tended to potentiate the action of vitamin C. These substances, which were extracted from red pepper and lemon, were shown by later chemical analysis to be members of a class of compounds called flavones or flavonols. When tested, they were found to decrease the breakage of small blood vessels, to prolong life in guinea pigs that had been deprived of vitamin C and to overcome small hemorrhages in human subjects who were vitamin C-deficient.[2]

This group of substances was later called vitamin P, referring to their effect on preventing small vessel or capillary permeability. None of them was later shown to have a true vitamin effect, however, in that deficiencies of them in the diet did not lead to an overt or diagnosable deficiency disease; and the designation of vitamin P was dropped in 1950 on the recommendation of the American Society of Biological Chemists and the American Institute of Nutrition.[3] Since that time, these substances—citrin, hesperidin, rutin, flavones and flavonols—have been termed *bioflavonoids* and have been found by a number of investigators, including Dr. Z. Zloch of Charles University in Czechoslovakia, to enhance the antiscorbutic activity of ascorbic acid.[4] According to Zloch, when bioflavonoids are administered with vitamin C, there is an increased uptake of the vitamin into the liver, kidney and adrenal glands, and protection of the vitamin C by the bioflavonoids, which seem to work as antioxidants—that is, preventing the destruction of C by its conversion to a less active form called dehydroascorbate. He also reported a greater decrease in blood cholesterol than in tests in which animals were treated with vitamin C alone.

Bioflavonoids are water-soluble substances associated

with colored materials that often but not always appear in fruits and vegetables as companions to vitamin C. Bioflavonoids were first found in the white segments of citrus fruits; there is ten times the concentration of bioflavonoids in the edible part of the fruit as is in the strained juice. Major natural sources of bioflavonoids include lemons, grapes, plums, black currants, grapefruit, apricots, buckwheat, cherries, blackberries and rose hips. Commercial methods of extracting bioflavonoids from the rinds of oranges, tangerines, lemons, limes, kumquats and grapefruits include those employing hot water or isopropanol. The antioxidant activity of bioflavonoids which protects vitamin C seems to result from their unique chemical structure; they act as reducing agents which are transported to the site where vitamin C is to be stored in the cell.[5]

RUTIN AND HESPERIDIN

Rutin is found in many plants. Buckwheat contains about 3 percent dry-basis rutin when the plant is starting to bloom. The rutin molecule is made up of a sugar half that makes the compound water-soluble and an antioxidant flavone half.

Hesperidin is the predominant flavonoid in lemons and sweet oranges. It is reasonably soluble in water and, like rutin, is made up of a sugar half attached to a flavone half. The chemical similarity of rutin and hesperidin indicates that both have a similar mode of action. Rutin is a slightly better reducing reagent than hesperidin.

Because bioflavonoids have not been identified as actual vitamins or essential nutrients, there is no Recommended Dietary Allowance (RDA) for them. This places the bioflavonoids in a class of substances known as accessory nutrients—nutrients which are therapeutically valuable for those whose biochemical individuality makes them essential.[6]

Since bioflavonoids occur with vitamin C only in natural food sources, synthetic vitamin C does not contain them unless they have been added by the manufacturer. Bioflavonoids have been found to be virtually nontoxic, because they are eliminated rapidly from the body by excretion after breakdown. Also, they will not cause yellowing of the skin, as does a high intake of carotene pigments from carrots and other red/orange-colored vegetables, even with consumption of fairly high doses.

QUERCETIN AND EPICATECHIN

Two flavonoids not found in foods but which have similar chemical structures to rutin and hesperidin are quercetin, which is derived by steam distillation of quercitrin bark, and epicatechin. These materials are also widely distributed in the plant kingdom, especially in the rinds and barks of wild fruits and trees, in clover blossoms and in ragweed pollen. They have been isolated from rhododendron, forsythia, hydrangea, pansies and eucalyptus. Considerable pharmacological research has been done on the use of these substances in the treatment of various medical problems. Doses of between 10 and 20 milligrams per day of quercetin have been used on patients who experience capillary fragility, easy bruising and small pin-point hemorrhages called petechiae. Quercetin has also been found to be a very powerful inhibitor of an enzyme called aldose reductase. The medical implications of this relationship will be discussed in a later section of this Guide dealing with bioflavonoids and diabetic cataracts.[7]

All these bioflavonoids have a very bitter taste and are therefore generally taken as supplements in timed-release tablets or in capsules that will not dissolve readily in the mouth.

BIOLOGICAL AND CLINICAL INVESTIGATIONS

Though a tremendous amount of work has been done with bioflavonoids, no deficiency state has ever been proven in animals or discovered in humans. Quercetin has been reported to have an inhibitory effect not only on aldose reductase, but on other enzymes such as histidine decarboxylase.[8] A number of reports have not shown any relationship between oral ingestion of the bioflavonoids and diminishment of capillary fragility. It is possible that the compound used in some of these experiments may not have been adequately absorbed from the intestinal tract. This seems to be one of the major problems with bioflavonoid preparations—inappropriate processing of the bioflavonoid can make it virtually unabsorbable. One of the major questions that needs to be asked about the therapeutic usefulness of bioflavonoids for nutritional supplementation is whether the supplement to be used has truly been demonstrated to be absorbable into the blood across the intestinal barrier. In the absence of such proof, the substance employed may do nothing but color the stool.

Work has been done to try to determine whether a bioflavonoid supplement is useful in preventing hemorrhages in the eye and in reducing the risk of stroke in susceptible patients. One report indicates a decreased incidence of hemorrhages of the retina and stroke in individuals who have taken bioflavonoid supplements,[9] although some other reports have not confirmed this observation.[10]

Beardwood and his associates have claimed that bioflavonoids are useful for preventing retinal damage in diabetics and for preventing bruising; however, these reports have not been confirmed by other investigators.[11]

It is clear from this brief summary that the history of the clinical and biological usefulness of bioflavonoids is clouded. There are many advocates of the therapeutic usefulness of bioflavonoids; others challenge their effectiveness. A review by Shils and Goodhart was published in 1956, discussing the pros and cons of bioflavonoid supplementation in nutritional medicine and confirming the controversial aspect of their usefulness.[12]

The following table lists the purported applications of bioflavonoid supplementation in the improvement of human functioning.

Purported Usefulness of Bioflavonoids as Food Supplements

Prevention of retinal hemorrhages
Reduction of capillary fragility (bruising)
Reduced risk of stroke in high blood pressure patients
Increased protection against arthritis, rheumatic fever
Reduced risk of arteriosclerosis
Decreased menopausal symptoms
Increased protection against oral herpes infection
Decreased risk of diabetic cataract
Decreased histamine response to allergen exposure
Prevention of habitual abortion
Reduction in ulcer problems
Treatment of dizziness due to inner ear problem
Decreased symptoms of asthma
Protection against radiation damage
Decreased inflammation after injury

RECENT DISCOVERIES ABOUT THE BIOFLAVONOIDS

Much of the history of the use of bioflavonoids as nutritional supplements has rested on their apparent ability to improve capillary wall integrity. The capillaries, or small blood vessels, must maintain a barrier between blood plasma and cells and the cellular environment. When the capillaries lose their integrity and become weakened, materials from the blood can penetrate into tissues, leading to easy bruising or hemorrhages, or substances can penetrate from the external environment through the intestinal tract or respiratory tract into the blood. When there is increased penetration of environmental substances into the body the symptoms of allergy or immune sensitivity can develop and the body's immune system can become sensitized to environmental agents. This may be the reason bioflavonoids have been suggested as useful in the management of asthma and stomach ulcers, as well as intestinal problems and some food allergies. The supplemental dose used in many of these clinical trials is between 500 and 3,000 milligrams a day of the citrus or buckwheat bioflavonoid complex, along with vitamin C at the same level. A stronger capillary wall prevents the invasion of the blood by foreign substances or the leakage of blood cells and plasma materials into tissues.

The role bioflavonoids play as protectors against vitamin C destruction may account for the way they guard capillaries against damage. The capillary walls are made up of a protein called collagen, which requires vitamin C for its synthesis; if the vitamin C in these cells is converted by oxidation to the dehydroascorbate, it is less active in its ability to stimulate the synthesis of collagen, which is used as the connective tissue to manufacture the capillary walls. Bioflavonoids seem to protect vitamin C from being converted to dehydroascorbate, and therefore may be very important in stimulating collagen synthesis and capillary wall integrity.

This favorable effect on collagen of the C-bioflavonoid complex has led to its suggested use for preventing viral infections or treating some forms of such infections. One recent relevant study deals with the common virus *herpes labialis*, which produces cold sores. These are generally self-limiting, and tend to get better by themselves in about nine and a half days. When only vitamin C was supplemented at 1000 mg per day, there was a slight reduction in the duration of the cold sores to approximately seven days. However, when vitamin C and bioflavonoids were administered together at levels of 1000 mg each, the length of time dropped from nine and a half to about three and a half days, which indicates that the vitamin C–bioflavonoid complex was extremely useful in helping the body defend itself against infection by the *herpes labialis* virus and was more effective than vitamin C by itself. This may be the result of the stimulating effect of the complex on collagen synthesis, which provides better protection against the infiltration of viruses.[13]

Another interesting study has recently demonstrated that vitamin C in combination with bioflavonoids and an oral proteolytic enzyme preparation containing chymotrypsin was more effective than nonsteroidal antiinflammatory drugs in reducing inflammation.[14] This may also be the result of strengthening the cells against agents which cause inflammation, or of some yet-to-be-understood role that bioflavonoids play in the immune mechanism. The level of bioflavonoids, vitamin C and proteolytic enzymes given to animals in this study is equivalent to a human dose of approximately 1000 mg of vitamin C, 500 mg bioflavonoids, and 25,000 units of chymotrypsin administered orally.[14]

A recent review of the physiological action of flavonoids shows a favorable effect on white blood cells in increasing immune defense, which may account for the antiinflammatory activity resulting from the oral supplementation.[15]

USE OF BIOFLAVONOIDS FOR DUODENAL ULCERS

Thirty-six cases of bleeding duodenal ulcers have been studied in relation to treatment with bioflavonoids and a low-acidity diet, compared to a group of patients on the same diet with no bioflavonoid supplementation. In the group given the supplements—500 mg of citrus bioflavonoids every six hours—the bleeding ceased on the fourth day. Continued supplementation with bioflavonoids and the bland diet led to healing of the intestinal mucosa and a normal duodenal contour after twelve to twenty-two days. There was no recurrence of bleeding after two years in twenty-three of the thirty-six cases. Twelve cases remained ulcer-free for one year or more, and the remaining cases were successfully treated with a second course of bioflavonoids; they were ulcer-free for four months. In the group that used the diet without bioflavonoids, less than 50 percent remained ulcer-free with continuation of the diet, and their improvement was much slower than it was in those who took the bioflavonoid supplement.[16]

EFFECTS ON THE PREVENTION OF DIABETIC CATARACT

One of the major complications of diabetes is a change in the opacity of the eye, leading to cataract. The mechanism by which cataract is generated in the eye has been studied extensively over the last few years and seems to relate to the activity of an enzyme in the eye called aldose reductase.[17] This enzyme is able to convert glucose in the eye into sugars such as sorbitol, which remain in the eye and crystallize out into the lens. In diabetics, this sorbitol attains a dangerously high level in the lens, which results in a change in the ability of the eye to transmit light and also produces excessive water retention, or what is called osmotic pressure, causing tissue damage. The sorbitol deposited in the eye does not come from dietary sources, but rather from the action of the enzyme aldose reductase converting blood sugar (glucose) to sorbitol. The reason the eye of the diabetic attracts a tremendous amount of sugar and activates this enzyme is that the lens, the nerves and the kidneys are insulin-insensitive tissues, which means that they take up sugar from the blood without the need of insulin. When the diabetic is unable to secrete enough insulin to take up more sugar from the blood into the other cells of the body such as muscle cells, the sugar is then driven into the eye by its high concentration in the blood and produces a significant elevation of its level in the lens, where it is converted from glucose to sorbitol by aldose reductase.

If this is the reason why diabetics get cataracts, then anything that can be done to either inhibit the aldose reductase or decrease the flow of sugar from the blood into the eye would help prevent them. One method of prevention is to regulate the blood sugar level of the diabetic through diet. This means using a higher-complex carbohydrate, lower-sugar and higher-fiber diet than is standard for the management of the diabetic patient.

Inhibition of aldose reductase would also prevent the build-up of sorbitol in the lens of the eye. A number of enzyme inhibitors have been studied in animals, and it has been found that they effectively delay the onset of cataract of diabetic subjects.[18]

Recently, it has been found that oral administration of quercetin, a known inhibitor of aldose reductase, leads to a significant decrease in the accumulation of sorbitol in the lens of diabetic animals, resulting in a delay in the onset of cataract if the bioflavonoid administration is continued.[19] The level of bioflavonoid given as an oral supplement in this study was very high, in human equivalents approximately 3000 to 7000 mg per day. The firm conclusion investigators made from their animal studies was that aldose reductase initiates the formation of cataract in diabetics and that the bioflavonoid aldose reductase inhibitor when given orally may be an effective preventive agent for cataract.

Studies are being continued to determine which flavonoids are most useful for the prevention of cataract and at what dose they would be most successful.[20] It is clear that when bioflavonoids are used for their pharmacological function as enzyme inhibitors, very high doses are required. These doses, on the order of thousands of milligrams per day, are far higher than normal dietary levels.

BIOFLAVONOIDS AS NUTRITIONAL SUPPLEMENTS: THE CONTROVERSY

It is apparent that bioflavonoids are not really a family of essential nutrients (substances required by all people on a daily basis, as are vitamins). The reason for this is that there are no acute deficiency symptoms when bioflavonoids are not included in the diet.

Their role is evidently that of accessory nutrients which potentiate the action of the antioxidant vitamin C and may have other potentiating effects. An accessory nutrient is a substance not considered essential for all individuals, but which may be required by some individuals to promote optimal function. Some examples of these are carnitine, taurine, octacosanol and dimethylglycine.

Bioflavonoids seem to fit this definition, since many individuals respond favorably to bioflavonoid supplementation, but not everyone requires them to maximize performance. Because of the controversy surrounding the use of nutrients as therapeutic agents, bioflavonoids have been discredited by many standard nutritionists as having no effective action. It should be recalled that many times the end of a story depends on its beginnings, and such may be the case with those who claim that bioflavonoids are not useful. If one assumes that the only use of trace nutrients such as vitamins and minerals is to prevent specific, definable deficiency diseases that occur in the absence of those nutrients, then it is true that bioflavonoids are not required in the diet. However, if one extends the definition of what is to be considered an important nutrient to include substances that enhance performance instead of simply preventing a deficiency disease, then bioflavonoids may be quite important for some individuals to achieve their best health.

There are still many nutritionists and medical people who believe that nutritive items are not useful in therapeutic doses, and therefore not needed as supplements beyond the average daily intake, particularly such substances as bioflavonoids, which have not been found useful as essential nutrients. There is a different, rapidly emerging school of thought which recognizes that many nutrients may be used as pharmacological agents. In amounts exceeding those which one would normally get in the diet, they may have profound, positive influences on physiological function that can help normalize people who have certain types of illness.[21]

This certainly seems to be the case with bioflavonoids; a wealth of clinical information and experimental data indicates their pharmacological impact in facilitating better vitamin C utilization and their roles in the reduction of capillary fragility, protection against viral infections, decreased inflammatory response and protection against diabetic cataracts. It is obvious that much more work needs to be done to identify the action of these substances in controlled human studies and to verify their clinical usefulness, but it is important to recognize that the therapeutic effectiveness of bioflavonoids has been reported for over fifty years, and as we learn more about their chemical structure and physiological action, it appears that the clinical testimonies have scientific foundation.

One other interesting reported use of bioflavonoids is in the amelioration of the symptoms of menopause, such as flushing or hot flashes and heart palpitations. Bioflavonoids have been reported at doses of 500 to 3000 mg per day, along with magnesium, vitamin B6 and vitamin E to control these menopausal symptoms successfully; however, no definite study has yet appeared as proof. Clinical observation precedes scientific investigation, so because it hasn't been proven doesn't necessarily mean it isn't correct. Future exploration of the relationship of bioflavonoid supplementation to the reduction of menopausal symptoms should settle the matter.

A very important characteristic of bioflavonoids is that they are naturally-occurring substances with virtually no toxicity and can thus be used safely. Dietary intake of bioflavonoids is quite high in those who eat oranges or grapefruit, including the white part next to the rind. Individuals who drink fruit juice and do not eat the whole fruit may get fair amounts of vitamin C, but not adequate levels of bioflavonoids. This would argue once again for eating foods that are as little processed as possible and as much in the natural state as possible.

It is also interesting to note that the amount of bioflavonoids required for optimal benefit in controlled studies seemed to be about equal to the amount of vitamin C used. This would mean that balances of bioflavonoids to vitamin C in therapeutic trials should be on the order of 1000 mg of the citrus or rutin bioflavonoids to 1000 mg of vitamin C. At this level there need be no worry of toxicity from either bioflavonoids or vitamin C, and therefore the risk of a clinical trial of these substances is negligible, while there is significant potential benefit, such as improvement of capillary-wall integrity and other positive physiological effects.

IS THERE A NEED FOR SUPPLEMENTATION?

Given these controversies, how might supplementation with bioflavonoids be considered clinically justifiable? There is uncertainty about the role bioflavonoids play in promoting health, and whether they are required nutrients in some individuals. It appears that the best way of identifying the therapeutic value of bioflavonoids and vitamin C is a clinical trial where there is no risk of toxicity and there is a potential significant benefit. Suitable subjects for such a clinical trial, in which vitamin C and bioflavonoids would be taken concurrently daily for two weeks to a month to see if any benefit results, would include individuals who bruise easily, have extensive muscle pain after contact sports, or those individuals who are at risk of stroke because of high blood pressure or of arteriosclerosis because of high blood cholesterol levels. It also would be indicated as a clinical trial for people who have symptoms of arthritis or significant allergies with advanced histamine response, including asthma. The literature is rich in reports of bioflavonoids and vitamin C being useful in wound healing, in protecting against various viral infections, including oral herpes, and in reduction of duodenal ulcer problems. Bioflavonoids have also been shown in a few clinical studies to help reduce the symptoms of menopause and prevent problems of habitual spontaneous abortion.[22]

Lastly, individuals who have diabetes and who should be protecting their eyes against cataract formation may want to use a clinical trial of vitamin C and bioflavonoids, as well as dietary modification to improve the management of blood sugar.

This range of clinical impacts of the use of bioflavonoids in conjunction with vitamin C indicates the potential therapeutic usefulness of this family of accessory nutrients. Because the benefits are potentially so significant and the toxic reactions negligible, it seems that the risk/benefit trade-off in a clinical trial of these substances would weigh heavily on the side of benefit for people displaying one or more of the symptoms discussed.

There is hope that in the future much more research will utilize the bioflavonoid complex and identify more completely the role of these substances at the cellular and physiological levels, so that their usefulness can be substantiated. Until then we must regard the bioflavonoid–substance P family as being an accessory group of nutritional substances which may in some individuals have very powerful therapeutic effects, and whose function appears to be protective against the cellular destruction of vitamin C, and which would therefore be suitable in a whole vitamin C complex supplementation program.

RECENT RESEARCH INTEREST

The past several years have witnessed a rekindled research interest in the bioflavonoid family of accessory nutrients. The citrus industry has long recognized the uniquely high concentrations of potassium, folic acid and vitamin C in citrus juice products but has only recently turned its attention to exploration of the biochemical functions of the concentrate of the white, soft, fleshy part of the fruit inside the rind, which is rich in bioflavonoids. This research has reconfirmed the value of bioflavonoids in the prevention of capillary fragility, and in the prevention of abnormal platelet adhesion ("sticky" blood cells) and reduction of inflammation.[23] The renewed interest in bioflavonoids by nutritional investigators will, we hope, delineate further the mechanisms of action of this family of accessory nutrients and will put their use on a more scientifically supportable basis.

Much of our present understanding of the role that therapeutic nutrition plays in improving health was born out of the clinical observations of practitioners. An example of this was the interesting observation made by John Ellis, M.D., practicing in a small Texas community, who reported that vitamin B6 in large quantities (10 to 20 times the Recommended Dietary Allowance) cured some patients with painfully swollen hands. It took some ten years to confirm this association by detailed scientific studies.[24]

This situation is like that of the bioflavonoids, where clinical associations have been made for years, but only recently are definitively controlled scientific studies being done to examine these observations critically. The preliminary data from these studies are most exciting, as they seem to confirm much of what has been previously observed as successful in bioflavonoid therapy.

NATURAL VERSUS SYNTHETIC NUTRIENTS

One topic that has generated considerable controversy in the nutritional supplement field is the difference between natural and synthetic nutrients. In general, there is no chemical difference between a naturally-derived vitamin B1 from yeast and a synthetically-derived vitamin B1 from petrochemical starting materials. They have the same chemical structure and they have the same physiological effects in the prevention of beri-beri. The same is true for all the other B-complex vitamins and vitamin C, but not for such nutrients as vitamin E, where there is a difference in chemical structure between the natural and synthetic forms of the vitamin.

The most interesting question is not the chemical structure of the nutrient in question but whether there is a difference between the benefits obtained from naturally-derived nutrients and those derived from a synthetic source. In a nutrient from a natural source, such as yeast or rose hips, there is a whole array of substances; some of them are known nutrients, such as vitamin C, and others may be trace substances of unknown chemical structure or physiological nature. This is certainly the case with vitamin C extracted from the whole grapefruit compared with synthetic vitamin C manufactured by chemical modification of corn sugar. Extraction from the whole grapefruit would not only provide ascorbic acid but might also provide a myriad of other substances, some of which may potentiate the activity of vitamin C. This is the case with the bioflavonoids, which are reported to potentiate the activity of vitamin C and would be found only in a naturally-derived vitamin C product (unless added to synthetically-derived vitamin C).

VITAMIN C METABOLITES AND BIOFLAVONOIDS

An exciting new suggestion has been made within the past few years concerning the therapeutic role that vitamin C may play in the activation of the immune system and in the prevention of such diseases as cancer. This suggestion is that vitamin C itself may not be the sole activating substance and that some of the metabolites of vitamin C, such as dehydroascorbate, isoascorbic acid, and other chemical substances that are derived from vitamin C in the human body, are involved.

Observations made by a number of investigators, and research by Dr. Constance Tsao at the Linus Pauling Institute of Science and Medicine in Palo Alto, California, have confirmed the fact that there are a number of trace metabolites of vitamin C present in biological samples and that some of these may actually have a more profound effect upon intracellular function than vitamin C itself. This may be the reason why some individuals, when given a large oral dose of vitamin C, excrete almost all of it unchanged in the urine, while others excrete only a small amount. Those people who have great need for vitamin C metabolites may actively convert the vitamin C itself into other substances which have profoundly beneficial cellular effects.

One of the metabolites of vitamin C which is known *not* to be beneficial is oxalic acid. It has been suggested that high-dose vitamin C therapy can increase urinary oxalate excretion and the consequent risk of kidney stones; however, work done during the last two years indicates that consumption of up to 10,000 milligrams of vitamin C a day by normal individuals on ordinary diets leads to no significant increase in oxalate output in the urine and, therefore, that the risk of kidney stones from vitamin C is minimal to nonexistent.

Bioflavonoids may play a role in this whole story of vitamin C metabolites because they are known to have an effect on the rate at which C is converted into its various metabolites; bioflavonoids are chemical reducing agents. If bioflavonoids do in fact help divide vitamin C into its metabolites in the tissues of the body, this would profoundly affect the cellular role of vitamin C in activating the immune system or repairing cells.

This may explain at the molecular level what is observed clinically: that bioflavonoids have been shown to improve the therapeutic action of vitamin C in some areas. It is exciting, since these observations of the effects of vitamin C metabolites on cellular function have opened the door to new types of studies which will examine the biochemical individualities of people in terms of their metabolism of vitamin C and relate that to their needs and functional capacities. Bioflavonoids deserve study in terms of the effect they may have on facilitating the metabolism of vitamin C and the improvement of health.

It is known that, in vitamin C-treated mice, the metabolite isoascorbic acid may have a different effect on cancer risk than vitamin C itself.[25] If bioflavonoids have an influence on the dissolution of vitamin C into its metabolites, then it is possible that these nutrient substances serve as potentiating agents for the effective functioning of vitamin C. This suggestion awaits further proof by detailed studies, but is certainly an interesting hypothetical explanation of the observed clinical benefits of bioflavonoids.

It is not clear whether everyone would benefit from taking bioflavonoids along with vitamin C for their synergizing ability. It is possible that certain individuals do not need the reducing-action effects of bioflavonoids for optimal activity of vitamin C as a nutrient, but in those individuals who may have specific cellular functional capacity which requires the bioflavonoids for protection of ascorbic acid and delivery of ascorbic acid metabolites in proper levels to tissues, this accessory nutrient would prove very useful.

If clinical symptoms of easy bruising, lowered immune defense or cataract formation continue while supplementing with straight vitamin C as ascorbic acid or ascorbate, it might be worthwhile to consider taking bioflavonoids along with the vitamin C.

It is important to recognize that the mention of bioflavonoids on the label of a supplement container does not guarantee that the product was from natural sources. Read the label carefully, keeping in mind that whatever is not clearly specified as being in the product probably is not. Also check the label for the bioflavonoid content, given in milligrams; the nearer to the vitamin C (ascorbic acid) content it is, the more natural the supplement's formulation is likely to be.

Also remember that some bioflavonoid preparations have been found to be virtually unabsorbable due to the way in which they were extracted from the natural product. Studies which demonstrate that the product that you are going to purchase has absorbable bioflavonoids are very important in helping you to determine the potential biological effects of the preparation. Manufacturers should be prepared to provide information concerning the absorbability and assimilability of bioflavonoids in their products.

CONCLUSION

It can be said that there is some apparent difference between natural and synthetic nutrients, taking into account the complex of accessory substances that result from the extraction of a natural product and the specific single nutritive substance resulting from manufacture from an isolated, purified starting material.

It is clear that bioflavonoids as a family come only from the extraction of natural products, and may be found either in the complex of naturally-derived vitamin C or added to the synthetically-derived vitamin C. Either of these preparations would provide therapeutically useful supplementation as long as the bioflavonoids were biologically absorbable.

The future of bioflavonoids as nutritional supplements depends upon the quality and direction of future research, but at this point it can be said that, from the clinical information available over the past thirty years, vitamin C, administered with bioflavonoids, appears to have therapeutic benefit above and beyond that of vitamin C by itself in many areas pertaining to capillary fragility and cellular function.

REFERENCES

1. Rusznyak, D. and Szent-Györgyi, A., *Nature 138:* 27 (1936).
2. Armentuno, P., Bentsath, M., Beres, B., and Szent-Györgyi, A., *Deut. Med. Wchnschr. 62:* 1325 (1936).
3. Joint Committee on Nomenclature: *Science 112:* 628 (1950).
4. Zloch, Z. *International J. Vit. Res. 39:* 269 (1969).
5. Scarborough, S. and Bacharach, T. *Vitamins and Hormones 8:* 1 (1949).
6. Bland, J., *Choline, Lecithin, Inositol, and Other "Accessory" Nutrients.* New Canaan, CT: Keats Publishing, 1982.
7. Underhill, L. *Can. J. Biochem. Physiol. 35:* 219 (1957).
8. Smyth, S., Lambert, M., and Martin, S. *Proc. Soc. Exp. Biol. Medicine 116:* 593 (1964).
9. Griffith, G., Krewson, L., and Naghiski, N. *Rutin and Related Flavonoids.* Easton, PA: Mack Publishing Co., 1955.
10. Schweppe, S. and Barker, T. *Amer. Heart J. 35:* 393 (1948).
11. Beardwood, A., Roberts, T., and Trueman, M. *Proc. Amer. Diabetes Assoc. 8:* 243 (1948).
12. Shils, S. and Goodhart, H. *The Flavonoids in Biology and Medicine.* New York: The National Vitamin Foundation, Inc. (1956).
13. Tengherdy, T. *Nutrition Reviews 36:* 10 (1978).
14. ———, *Arzneim-Forsch. Drug Res. 27:* 6 (1977).
15. Review: "Action of Flavonoids on Blood Cells," *International J. Vit. Res. 44:* (1974).
16. Weiss, S., Weiss, J., and Weiss, B. *Amer. J. of Gastroenterology 34:* 726 (1958).
17. Kinoshita, J.H. *Opthalmol. 13:* 713 (1974).
18. Dvornik, D., Krami, M., and Kinoshita, J.H. *Science 182:* 1146 (1973).
19. Varma, S.D., Mixuno, A., and Kinoshita, J.H. *Science 195:* 205 (1977).
20. Varma, S.D. and Kinoshita, J.H. *Biochim. Biophys. Acta 338:* 632 (1974).
21. Spiller, A. *Nutritional Pharmacology.* New York: A.R. Liss, 1982.

22. Jacobs, A. *Surg. Gynec. and Obstet. 103:* 233 (1956).

23. Robbins, R.C. "Medical and Nutritional Aspects of Citrus Bio-flavonoids" in *Citrus Nutrition and Quality*, F. Nagy and J.A. Attaway, eds. Washington, DC: Symposium Series 143, American Chemical Society, 1980.

24. Ellis, J., Folkers, K., Watanabe, T., and Wood, F.F. "Clinical Results of a Cross-over Treatment with Pyridoxine and Placebo of the Carpal Tunnel Syndrome." *Amer. J. Clin. Nutr. 32:* 2040 (1979).

25. Tsao, C., and Pauling, L. "The Effect of Isoascorbic Acid-Treated Mice." *International Journal for Vitamin and Nutrition Research*, accepted for publication.

- **Herbs and Herbal Medicine** by William H. Lee, R.Ph., Ph.D.
- **How to Cope with Menstrual Problems—A Wholistic Approach** by Nikki Goldbeck
- **Hypoglycemia** by Marilyn Light
- **Kelp, Dulse and Other Sea Supplements** by William H. Lee, R.Ph., Ph.D.
- **Lysine, Tryptophan and Other Amino Acids** by Robert Garrison, Jr., R.Ph., M.A.
- **The Mineral Transporters** by William H. Lee, R.Ph., Ph.D.
- **Nutrition and Exercise for the Over 50s** by Susan Smith Jones, Ph.D.
- **Nutrition and Stress** by Harold Rosenberg, M.D.
- **A Nutritional Guide for the Problem Drinker** by Ruth Guenther, Ph.D.
- **Nutritional Parenting** by Sara Sloan
- **Octacosanol, Carnitine and Other "Accessory" Nutrients Vol. 2** by Jeffrey Bland, Ph.D.
- **Propolis: Nature's Energizer** by Carlson Wade
- **Spirulina** by Jack Joseph Challem
- **A Stress Test for Children** by Jerome Vogel, M.D.
- **Tofu, Tempeh, Miso and Other Soyfoods** by Richard Leviton
- **Vitamin B3 (Niacin)** by Abram Hoffer, M.D., Ph.D.
- **Vitamin C Updated** by Jack Joseph Challem
- **Vitamin E Updated** by Len Mervyn, Ph.D.
- **The Vitamin Robbers** by Earl Mindell, R.Ph., Ph.D. and William H. Lee, R.Ph., Ph.D.
- **Wheat, Millet and Other Grains** by Beatrice Trum Hunter